Dedication:
To those that care,
To help us grow

Visit the curious duo online:
www.mikeyandotis.com

Instagram - mikeyandotis

Copyright © 2019 by Mr. Ray Ray
Illustrations by Heather Workman

All rights reserved. No part of this book may be reproduced or used in any manner withoutwritten permission of the copyright owner except for the use of quotations in a book review.

ISBN: 978-1-7331631-0-1 (hardback)
ISBN: 978-1-7331631-1-8 (e-book)
ISBN: 978-1-7331631-2-5 (paperback)

Published by Fun Family Publishing
www.funfamilypublishing.com

THE ADVENTURES OF MIKEY & otis

By Mr. Ray Ray + His Friends

As Mikey woke up and stretched his fuzzy paws, he noticed Mom was in a hurry to get ready.

"What will today bring?" He wondered.

Mikey started to imagine what the day had in store for him.

Mom packed all kinds of items in the car. Then they were off, off, and away!

Mom drove until Mikey, using his extra powerful senses, smelled planes—lots of them— and realized he was at the airport.

"Oh no, is Mom leaving on a trip?" Mikey began to worry, but his mood quickly changed: "Wait! Grandma and Grandpa are meeting us here. This is turning out to be a great day!"

Mom, Grandma, and Grandpa headed into the building. Mikey, watching from the car, saw tons of boxes and packages.

"Could it be a new toy for me?" Mikey wondered. "Grandma and Grandpa always bring me new toys!"

Meanwhile, Otis woke up from his airplane ride to a lady picking him up and thought, "Who is this? Where are we going? That was not the fun ride I was promised."

When Mikey and Otis first laid eyes on each other, they were both surprised and confused.

Otis **OINKED** to Mikey, "Please don't eat me!"

Mikey snapped back, "My toys don't talk. What is going on here?!"

He wanted nothing to do with this new addition to the family.

They arrived at a cool-looking building in the city, and went up a magical device that popped them to the top with a DING!

The ride excited Otis. And this new lady seemed nice; he might just like his new home after all.

When Otis trotted through the front door, he couldn't believe what he saw: "Oh wow! And a bed with a view!"

He jumped toward a pile of toys.

Mikey was not amused: "Hey, little man, don't touch that ball; it's mine!" Suddenly Mikey heard the sound of keys and rushed to the door.

After hugging Mikey, Dad came to offer a welcoming ear scratch. Otis liked Dad!

Feeling tired, Otis went to bed, along with everyone else in his new home.

That night, Otis was restless and did not sleep much. Hearing his sniffles, Mom stayed up with him all night.

She told Otis bedtime stories to help him sleep.

Poor Otis had no choice but to watch from his pen.

However, when friends came over, the tables turned! Otis got all the attention and loved every moment of it.

Otis was becoming the star of the house. Mikey didn't like it one bit.

It seemed like the new brothers might never get along!

Mikey kept dodging his brother from outside his pen and Otis kept hogging all the attention.

But then, all that changed the day The Neighborhood Cats showed up.

"Well, hellloooooo there new guy," the cats meowed cooly through the window.

"What a tasty-looking piggy!" said the large cat, batting the window open and licking his lips.

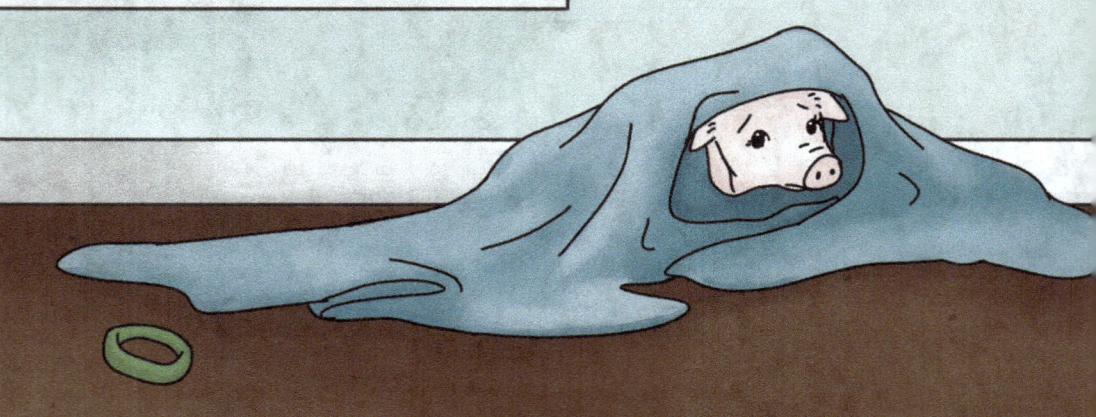

Then suddenly, Otis heard a loud bark from the next room and his heart leapt with hope. Could it be...?

As he was turning to leave, Otis caught Mikey's eye. Otis, with a big smile and an **OINK**, said, "Thanks, bro."

"Duh," shrugged Mikey. "That's what brothers are for, nobody teases my bro. Well...nobody but me." Then, Mikey grinned too.

Over the next weeks, Otis and Mikey played games and enjoyed music and movies together.

They were not just brothers...they were becoming best friends.

It didn't take long before Otis and Mikey were coordinating their outfits and causing all kinds of sass together.

www.ingramcontent.com/pod-product-compliance
Lightning Source LLC
Chambersburg PA
CBHW051431070526
44584CB00023B/3673